W9-CHO-035

J GN
DISNEY
05/07

Walt Disney's Comics and Stories
No. 664, January 2006
Published monthly by Gemstone Publishing,
© 2006 Disney Enterprises, Inc., except where noted.
All rights reserved. Nothing contained herein may be reproduced
without the written permission of Disney Enterprises, Inc.,
Burbank, CA., or other copyright holders.

ISBN 1-888472-17-0

OH YEAH? THEN WHAT MADE **THESE** TRACKS?

WOW! THEY DO LOOK LIKE BEAR TRACKS, DON'T THEY?

IT DOESN'T MAKE SENSE! WHY WOULD A BEAR BE OUT IN WEATHER LIKE THIS?

MAYBE IT'S A PRANKSTER!

IF IT IS, HE'S WEARING ONE WHACKING BIG **FUR COAT!** LOOK!

IT **IS** A BEAR, AND HE'S REALLY MOVING!

ODD! ALMOST LIKE HE'S RUNNING AWAY FROM SOMETHING!

WELL IT CERTAINLY ISN'T FROM **US!**

QUICK, LOUIE, GET A SHOT OF IT!

YOU'D BETTER HAVE PLENTY OF FILM BOYS! LOOK WHAT'S COMING!

UH, OH! I JUST REMEMBERED! ACCORDING TO THE JUNIOR WOODCHUCKS GUIDEBOOK, THIS IS AN AREA WHERE THERE HAVE BEEN SIGHTINGS OF THE **SASQUATCH!**

SASQUATCH? YOU MEAN ONE OF THOSE ABOMINABLE SNOWMAN TYPES?

PRETTY MUCH! MOST PEOPLE CONSIDER IT MORE OF A **LEGEND** THAN A REALITY!

NO LEGEND MADE THESE TRACKS, BOYS! LET'S FOLLOW THEM AND GET FAMOUS!

WHAT DO YOU MEAN, **FAMOUS**?

WE'RE GOING TO **PHOTOGRAPH A SASQUATCH!**

BUT ALAS—

THE TRACKS JUST **END!** HOW CAN SUCH A THING BE?

IT **BACKTRACKED!** THERE ISN'T ANY OTHER EXPLANATION!

AND WE DIDN'T SEE ANY INDICATION OF WHERE IT LEFT ITS TRACK, EITHER!

THIS SASQUATCH IS A CLEVER FELLOW!

NOT CLEVER ENOUGH TO FOX **ME** AGAIN! THIS TIME **WE'LL** BE CLEVER AND LEAD THIS GUY INTO A **TRAP!**

WHAT SORT OF TRAP?

WE DIG A HOLE IT CAN FALL INTO!

GET REAL, UNCA DONALD! THE SASQUATCH MAY BE **EIGHT FEET TALL!**

WE'D HAVE TO DIG A **MINE SHAFT!**

OR CENTURIES, PEOPLE HAVE WISHED THEY COULD CONTROL THE WEATHER—

SIGH! I'M AFRAID THIS WINTER *WALK* IN THE WOODS JUST ISN'T THE SAME WITHOUT *SNOW!*

SO WHAT? LOOK, I THINK I FOUND AN OLD *PATH!* STOP BEING A *GRUMP* AND *ENJOY* THE DAY!

D 98103

I *SHOULD*, MINNIE! BUT I LOVE SNOW, AND I *HATE WAITING* FOR IT ALL YEAR! I WISH IT WOULD SNOW *ALL* THE TIME!

CAREFUL WHAT YOU WISH FOR, MICKEY MOUSE! YOU MIGHT *GET* IT!

WOULD *THAT* BE SO BAD?

HEY, AN OLD *SHACK* IN THE MIDDLE OF NOWHERE!

HOW'D IT GET COVERED IN *ICE* LIKE THAT? LET'S GO TAKE A *LOOK!*

THANK HEAVEN HE ISN'T FOLLOWING US!

WHEN YOU CAN THROW *CARS* AROUND, WHY BOTHER WITH TITCHY *HUMANS?*

OH, NO — HERE'S CLARABELLE'S *ADDRESS,* BUT THE *HOUSE* IS GONE!

NO! IT'S LOST SOMEWHERE *UNDER* ALL THAT *SNOW!*

WELL, WE'VE GOTTA *SAVE* MOUSETON BEFORE THE SNOW BEAST DOES ANY MORE DAMA—

GRACIOUS, YOU SHOULDA *CALLED* FIRST! I'M AFRAID THE HEAT'S OUT AND IT ISN'T VERY *COMFORTABLE* HERE!

*M*ICKEY EX-PLAINS HIS PRE-DICAMENT—

ARE YOU SURE YOU WANT ME TO TRANSLATE *THIS?* IT'S NOT VERY *GOOD* POETRY — MAYBE YOU'D RATHER HEAR SOME OF *MINE!*

JUST *TRANSLATE,* CLARABELLE!

NO NEED TO BE *RUDE!*

THE DIARY *ALSO* SAYS YOU HAVE TO HOLD THE *BOX— OPEN*—TOWARD THE BEAST'S *FACE* FOR THE INCANTATION TO WORK!

NOW HOW DO I GET *UP* TO HIS *FACE?*

DON'T COME GAWKIN' TO ME! *YOU RELEASED* THE DARN MONSTER—*YOU* FIGURE IT OUT!

FOUR-LEGGED FUR-BEARERS... FRIENDS OR FOES? IN THE DUCK FAMILY, OPINIONS DIFFER...

IT'S A *PROBLEM!*

WE KEEP STRAY CRITTERS BY THE DOZEN, AND UNCA DONALD LIKES 'EM NO WAY, NOHOW!

D97198

HE WAS HOPPING MAD OVER THAT *BEAVER* IN THE WOODSHED!

DUCKBURG WELLS

THEN OUR *MOLE* WOLFED DOWN HIS BEGONIAS!

IT'S NEW YEAR'S EVE! TIME TO WASH OUR GOOD NAMES CLEAN!

HEAR! HEAR! BUT *HOW?*

WITH A *RESOLUTION!* WE MUST SEND OUR PETS *BACK* TO THE *WILD*— FREE EVERY BIRD, BEAST, AND COCKROACH!

KEEP A STIFF UPPER BEAK, MEN! IT'S WHAT *MUST* BE DONE!

IT'S A *NEW YEAR,* AND A *NEW BROOM* SWEEPS CLEAN! ⇒SIGH!⇐

THE BOYS MAY HAVE THE RIGHT IDEA! FOR UNCLE DONALD IS CERTAINLY TIRED OF ANIMALS!

"CIRCUS'S FINAL SHOW IN TOWN TO BOAST COUNTRY'S LARGEST MENAGERIE!"

COUNTRY'S LARGEST? MY NEPHEWS HAVE BROKEN THAT RECORD!

IT'S A WONDER I DON'T INHALE THEIR PETS WITH EVERY BREATH

HOLY TOLEDO!

THAT'S THE LIVING END! I'LL TURN YOU INTO SUCCOTASH, YOU GLORIFIED CROW!

CRACK!

OH, MY GOODNESS!

I WAS GONNA SUCCOTASH YOU! BUT SUDDENLY I DON'T FEEL LIKE IT!
=GULP!=

I GUESS PETS DON'T KNOW WHEN THEY'RE MAKING TROUBLE! IT'S TIME I FIGURED THAT OUT AND CANNED THE GRIPING!

I'LL GET ALONG BETTER WITH ANIMALS FROM THIS DAY FORWARD! IT'S NEW YEAR'S EVE AND THAT'S MY RESOLUTION!

YEAH! I'LL LET SOME *AFFECTIONATE* CRITTER INTO THE HOUSE— THE KIND THE KIDS WON'T BE ABLE TO SHOO OUT SO *EASILY!*

THEY WON'T BE ABLE TO GET RID OF HIM! THEY'LL *PLEAD* WITH ME FOR MERCY! ⇒*HEH-HEH!*⇐ NOW TO FIND AN ANIMAL...

RUE MORGUE PET PALACE

OOK!

BINGO!

DOES YOUR APE LIKE KIDS, MA-DOM?

CAGLIOSTRO? SURE! BUT HE DOESN'T LIKE BANANAS, SO I'M SELLING HIM *CHEAP...* $600!

...$600!... Um... CAN'T I SORTA *RENT* HIM ON A *TRIAL* BASIS?

EASY AS PIE, DUCK!

AFTER I CLOSE AT 8 TONIGHT I'M OFF ON VACATION! BUT BRING CAGLIOSTRO BACK BEFORE THEN, AND THE $600 IS YOURS AGAIN!

SWELL! I'VE GOT PLENTY OF TIME TO PULL THE GAG, RETURN THE APE, AND GET MY MONEY BACK!

COME ON HOME TO MY CASTLE, CAGLIOSTRO! WE'LL SOON HAVE THINGS MOVING IN JUNGLE RHYTHM!

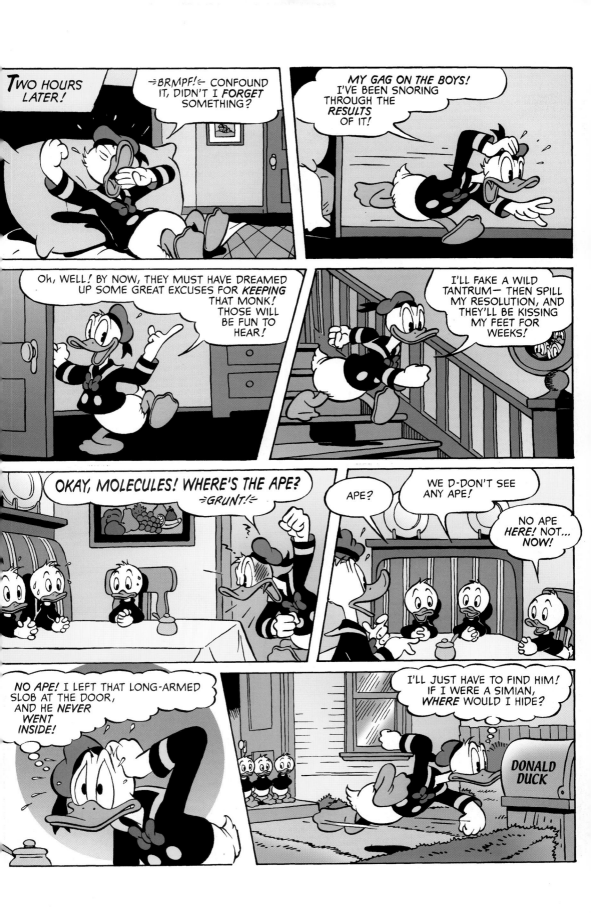

WE LEARNED SIGN LANGUAGE IN THE JUNIOR WOODCHUCKS! WE CAN SIGNAL THOSE HAIRY THUGS TO *STOP!*

NOT SO FAST!

IF WE CALL OFF THE APES, WILL YOU *STOP BLAMING US KIDS* FOR WHAT HAPPENED TODAY?

SCOUT'S HONOR! ⇒GASP!⇐ THAT IS... YES! YES!

SO DONALD—AND HIS MONEY—ARE RESCUED!

YOU'RE PRETTY SOURED ON ANIMALS AFTER ALL THAT, HUH, UNCA DONALD?

⇒SNORT!⇐

HOW'S ABOUT A *RESOLUTION COMPROMISE?* WE KEEP THE *NEXT* CRITTER WE SEE, AND NO MORE!

INFANTS, IT'S A DEAL!

THE NEXT CRITTER YOU— OH, *MY HEAVENLY DAYS!*

OKAY, BOYS, *OUR DEAL* SAYS HE'S *YOURS!* BUT WOULDN'T YOU RATHER HAVE A *GUINEA PIG?* OR A *MOUSE?* OR A FROG OR A HAMSTER OR...

SURE, UNCA DONALD! HAPPY NEW YEAR!

NEW YEAR'S COSTUME PARTY

The End.

LATER...

OH, DEAR! THE *FIRST* RESOLUTION IS BROKEN ALREADY!

POP JUST THREW HIS CLOTHES AROUND WHEN HE CAME IN LAST NIGHT!

AND HE PROMISED TO GET UP EARLIER IN THE MORNING, TOO!

I KNOW HE'LL WANT ME TO HELP HIM KEEP HIS RESOLUTIONS!

POP, IT'S NEW YEAR'S DAY... AND I WAS THINKING...

WELL, DON'T! GO 'WAY! LEAVE ME BE!

GOSH! POP WAS OUT LATE, AND HE'S KIND OF TOUCHY!

SEEMS STRANGE THAT HE WOULD BRING A *HORN* HOME WITH HIM!

YEAH! THAT'S WHUT'S GOT ME WORRIED!

MAW'S ALWAYS GOT TO HAVE HER LITTLE JOKES! IF I COULD ONLY *FIND OUT* WHAT TH' BIG PRIZE WUZ...

THEN I'D KNOW IF IT WUZ WORTHWHILE KEEPIN' MY NEW YEAR'S RESOLUTIONS!

THERE'S *ONE WAY* O' FINDIN' OUT! I'LL *TRICK* MAW INTO TELLIN' ME!

G'MORNIN', MAW!

WHY, 'ZEKIAL! WHAT A NICE SURPRISE! HAPPY NEW YEAR!

IT'S SO NICE TO SEE YOU *UP EARLY*, TOO! COME IN!

ARE YOU KEEPING ALL YOUR RESOLUTIONS?

OH, SURE!

HOW ABOUT THE ONE ABOUT QUARRELING?

THAT ONE'S *EASY!* I AIN'T SEEN ANBODY YET TO QUARREL WITH!

THAT'S GRAND, ZEKE! AND HERE'S SOME BEAUTIFUL LITTLE GOLD STARS FOR YOU! AREN'T YOU HAPPY?

OH, YEAH... SURE MAW! I JEST *LOVES* 'EM!

AT THIS RATE, IT WON'T BE LONG BEFORE I GIT THAT... ER...

NOW, DON'T TEASE! I'M *NOT* GOING TO TELL YOU WHAT IT IS YET!

BUT, IF YOU WANT TO WIN ANOTHER GOLD STAR, I'VE GOT SOME *WINDOWS TO BE WASHED!*

HUH?

GAWSH, MAW! THAT'S A SHAME... I JEST REMEMBERED I GOT AN IMPORTANT ENGAGEMENT!

WOW! WHAT A NARRER ESCAPE!

I SHOULDA KNOWN BETTER'N T'GO OVER TO MAW'S! I'LL *SEND* LI'L WOLF!

LISSUN, SON... I WANT **YOU** TO GO OVER TO GRANDMAW'S AN' SEE IF **YOU** KIN FIND OUT ABOUT THAT BIG PRIZE!

I DON'T THINK SHE'LL TELL ME, POP!

FIDDLE STICKS! SHE'LL NEVER SUSPECT THAT **I** SENT YA!

JEST DROP IN LIKE YA WUZ MAKIN' A FRIENDLY CALL!

IF SHE'S GOT ANY WORK T'BE DONE... IT MIGHT **HELP** GIT TH' ANSWER OUTA HER!

OKAY, POP!

WHILLIKERS! POP WORKS HARDER **AVOIDING** WORK THAN HE WOULD WORKING!

HELLO, GRANDMA!

WHY... HELLO, LI'L WOLF!

PSHAW! I'M DISAPPOINTED IN YOUR FATHER!

WHY, GRANDMA?

I FIGURED HE'D WAIT A **LITTLE LONGER** BEFORE HE SENT YOU OVER!

MUCH LATER!

IT'S ALMOST TOO SCARY TO COMPREHEND! I'LL ACTUALLY HAVE TO *GET A JOB* LIKE *NORMAL* PEOPLE!

HAPPY BEGGIN', BUD!

-≻EH?≺-

plonk!

A *PENNY!* A *PENNY* POLLUTES THE HAT INTO WHICH TWO MILLION BUCKS ONCE FELL!

I'LL THROW THIS *INSULT* INTO DAVY JONES' LOCKER!

WAIT!

LET ME *SEE* THAT PENNY BEFORE YOU GET *RID* OF IT, MAN!

YEP! THAT'S JUST THE COIN I *THOUGHT* IT WAS!

A GRUNGY OLD PENNY! AND?

AND IT'S A *1787 NEW YORK STATE CENT*, THE *THREE*-MILLION-DOLLAR RARITY I'VE SPENT *TEN* YEARS *LOOKING* FOR!

-≻GURGLE-URP!≺-

SO...

IMAGINE, *ME* LOSING *FAITH* IN MY LUCK! IT'S TIME I *ATE CROW...* ...*AFTER* THE *COQ AU VIN*, OF COURSE! TO THE RESTAURANT, BOYS!

YESSIR!

The End

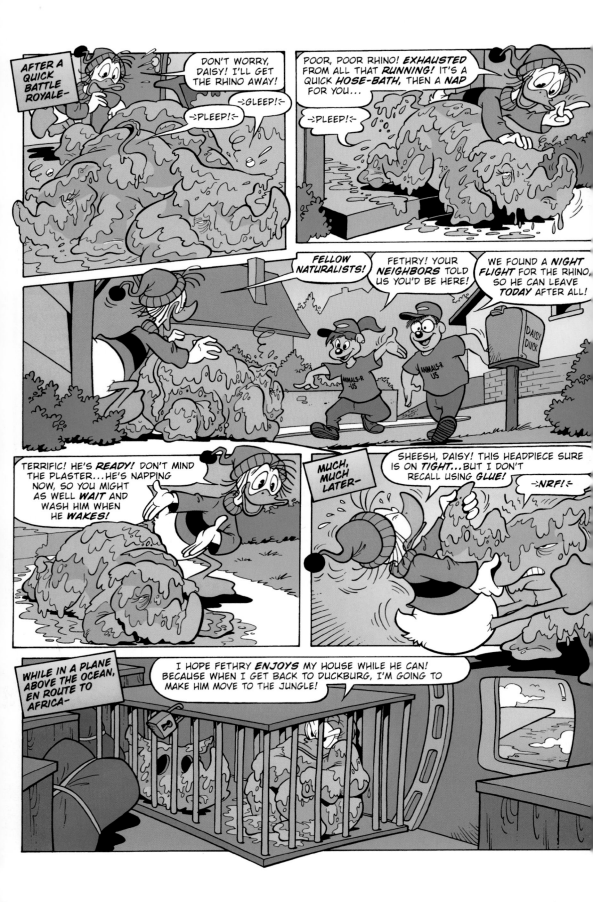

WALT DISNEY'S

DONALD DUCK in

THE MAGNIFICENT SEVEN
(minus 4)
CABALLEROS

THE THREE CABALLEROS IN BRAZIL! DONALD DUCK HAS FLOWN TO *RIO DE JANEIRO* AND MET UP WITH HIS TWO OLD PALS— *JOSÉ CARIOCA* (WHOSE HOMETOWN IS RIO!) AND *PANCHITO PISTOLES* FROM MEXICO!

MEETING ATOP THE SCENIC "SUGAR LOAF MOUNTAIN," THE THREE COMPADRES HAVE DECIDED THEY NEED *ADVENTURE* TO PEP UP THEIR DULL AND DEPRESSING LIVES!

D 2004-032

AT JOSÉ'S SUGGESTION, THEY HAVE BECOME *GARIMPEIROS*— *DIAMOND PROSPECTORS* IN THE *MATO GROSSO*, THE INTERIOR PLATEAU REGION OF BRAZIL!

TO HELP HIM ON HIS ADVENTURE, DONALD'S NEPHEWS HAVE ARRANGED TO LEND HIM A *JUNIOR WOODCHUCK PAMPHLET* ALL ABOUT BRAZIL! IT'S NOTHING LIKE A *REAL* WOODCHUCK GUIDEBOOK, BUT IT AIN'T BAD!

SO THE THREE CABALLEROS HAVE SET OUT ACROSS THE SWAMPS AND GRASSLANDS OF THE *MATO GROSSO* ON A *HORSE*, A *LLAMA*, AND AN *OX*!

READY FOR WHATEVER HIGH ADVENTURE COMES THEIR WAY...

...THE THREE CABALLEROS RIDE AGAIN!

WELL... ER... THINGS SURELY GET BETTER THAN THIS! LET'S HAVE A LOOK—

WHAT IS THIS STRANGE TREE? IS IT GROWING *COCONUTS*?

NO, WE HAVE THOSE IN RIO! WE CALL IT A *CANNONBALL TREE* BECAUSE OF THOSE HARD FRUITS!

WHAP!

ÓTIMO! THIS IS LIKE A NATURE STUDY PROGRAM! NOW DONALDO SHOWS US A BRAZILIAN *ANACONDA*!

MUY BUENO!

ARE THOSE NOT *DANGEROUS*?

QUE NADA — THAT IS A *TINY* ONE! THERE ARE TALES THAT EXPLORERS HAVE SEEN ANACONDAS 20 OR *30* METERS LONG!

CARAMBA! THAT ONE IS BIG *ENOUGH!* I'M GLAD DONAL' HAS A TIGHT *GRIP* ON IT!

WHAT *ELSE* CAN YOU TELL YOUR *EAGER* STUDENTS, PANCHITO AND JOSÉ, OF THAT SPECIMEN, PROFESSOR DONALDO?

I ⟫GASP!⟫ CAN TELL YOU ⟫GASP!⟫ I'M LUCKY THAT HE WASN'T *HUNGRY!*

AH! YOU REMIND MY STOMACH — WE HAVE NOT HAD *BREAKFAST* YET!

SÍ! LET US LOOK FOR FRUIT IN THE WOODS!

THERE ARE SO MANY WONDERFUL ANIMALS IN BRAZIL! HUMMINGBIRDS! MONKEYS! *MUITO* TYPES OF BEAUTIFUL PARROTS! JAGUARS! BUT THEY GROW *FEWER* EVERY YEAR!

SÍ! I HEAR THAT *74,000 ACRES* OF FOREST IS *DESTROYED* EVERY DAY IN BRAZIL!

AND THERE ARE ALSO *EVIL* MEN WHO *TRAP* THE WILD ANIMALS AND *SELL* THEM ILLEGALLY TO *STUPID* PEOPLE!

WHOOPS! WATCH OUT FOR THIS *PIT*!

LOOK! AN ANIMAL HAS *FALLEN* IN!

MERDA! THAT IS JUST WHAT I SAY! IT IS A *PITFALL TRAP* OF THE STEALERS OF WILD ANIMALS!

WHIMPER...

TOO BAD! BUT WHAT CAN *WE* DO?

UH... NO KIDDING, FELLAS! I WANT TO GET *OUT* OF HERE!

THAT DONAL' IS IMPATIENT FOR THE *ACTION!*

OHO! HE WILL SOON BE *HAPPY!* THE TRAPPER ALREADY RETURNS!

CARAMBA! IT IS A WHOLE BAND OF *INDIANS!* I THINK WE ARE OUTNUMBERED...?

›SH!‹ LET'S SEE HOW *DONALDO* HANDLES THEM!

›ULP!‹ HIYA, FELLAS! SHRUNK ANY NICE HEADS LATELY?

HEY! PUT ME *DOWN!* I'M NOT ONE OF YOUR DARN *JUMBO MICE!*

DONAL' IS GOING *WITH* THEM! LET US GET THE MOUNTS AND FOLLOW QUIETLY!

@#%@☆!!!

DONAL' IS USING MORE OF THOSE *EXOTIC WORDS!*

YES, I THINK HE'S SPEAKING TO THEM IN AN *INDIAN DIALECT!*

PANCHITO AND JOSÉ FOLLOW THE INDIANS FOR SOME DISTANCE THROUGH PLAINS AND MARSHES—

@#%@A!!!

NTIL FINALLY—

THEY WENT INTO THAT *HUT!*

THEY ARE *DEFINITELY* ILLEGAL TRAPPERS! LOOK AT ALL THE POOR BIRDS AND BEASTS IN THE CAGES AND PENS!

WHAT HAVE YOU IDIOT SAVAGES BROUGHT ME *NOW?*

WE THINK HIM NAMED @#%@☆!!!

THAT WHAT HIM SAY PLENTY MUCH!

COOL! IT'S NICE TO HAVE A *GUEST,* EVEN ONE WHO TEACHES SUCH LANGUAGE TO MY *SUBJECTS!*

GET US COLD SODAS FROM THE STREAM!

YES, CHIEF!

THUD

YOU'RE AN INDIAN CHIEF?

YEAH... WHEN MY *POP* WAS CHIEF, HE SENT ME TO BE *EDUCATED* IN CIVILIZATION! I WAS *KICKED OUTTA* HALFA DOZEN COLLEGES!

HOW COULD AN INDIAN *AFFORD* THAT?

AH, BUT POP KNEW THE SECRET OF THE *"MINES OF FEAR"*! OUR TRIBE SUPPOSEDLY DISCOVERED THE *"SHINING ROAD"* TO THE *CRYSTAL CITY* OVER 200 YEARS AGO!

THE *"MINES OF FEAR"*?

SOMETHING LIKE THAT! IT'S A LOTTA *HOOEY*, BUT THE OLD BOY *DID* HAVE A SOURCE FOR *GEMS*! HE USED THEM TO PAY FOR SENDING ME TO LEARN *MEDICINE* AND *SCIENCE* "FOR THE GOOD OF OUR PEOPLE" — YOU KNOW, THOSE MANGY SAVAGES OUTSIDE!

GENERATOR

HA! IN CIVILIZATION, WHAT I LEARNED WAS *GREED* AND *AVARICE*!

YOU BECAME A *LAWYER*?

NO, NO, NO, I MEAN I LEARNED HOW NICE IT IS TO HAVE *MONEY* TO SPEND IN THE BIG CITES! I CAME BACK ONLY TO FIND OUT *POP'S SECRET*, BUT HE *NEVER TOLD ME*, CURSE HIM!

GOOD FOR POP!

NOW I'M STUCK IN THIS *DUMP*! ALL I HAVE LEFT OF POP'S GEMS IS THIS *CHIEF'S NECKLACE*, BUT IT'S NOT ENOUGH FOR LIVING LONG IN A NEW YORK OR LAS VEGAS MANSION!

I'LL *FIND* THOSE HIDDEN MINES SOMEDAY! MEANWHILE, NOW THAT I'M CHIEF, I *FORCE* MY STUPID BROTHERS TO *TRAP ANIMALS* TO SELL TO WHOMEVER PAYS *CASH*!

YOU'RE A REAL *CHARM-BOY*!

WELL, THANKS FOR THE SODA! I NEED TO HEAD BACK TO CAMP!

OH, SORRY! DID I FAIL TO MENTION THE *OTHER* ILLEGAL BUSINESS I DABBLE IN BESIDES ANIMAL SALES? IT'S *PEOPLE SALES*!

WUH-OH! I DON'T LIKE WHERE THIS IS GOING...

YEAH, ANYTIME I GLOM ONTO A GRINGO TOURIST, I HOLD HIM FOR *RANSOM*!

≥GULP!≤

SO, SIT AND *RELAX*, BUDDY! YOU *CAN'T ESCAPE*! THE FRONT DOOR IS GUARDED!

MAYBE HE'LL USE THE *BACK* DOOR!

?

FORGET IT! THERE *AIN'T NO* BACK DOOR!

HUH? WHO--

SURE THERE IS, AMIGO! RIGHT *BEHIND* YOU!

CRASH!

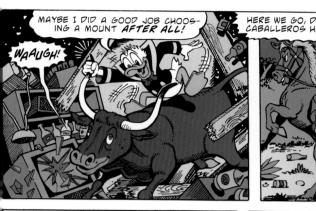

HEY, YOU FUZZY GUYS ARE *TOO SLOW!* YOU'LL NEVER GET AWAY! BETTER *CLIMB ABOARD!*

~NAGH! NAGH!~

ANOTHER INDIAN NAME? WE CALL THEM *SLOTHS!*

VAMANOS, MUCHACHOS!

HEY! THOSE DO-GOODERS SWIPED MY *NECKLACE!* IT'S WORTH THOUSANDS OF BUCKS!

...NOT TO MENTION IT'S THE *TRIBAL AMULET OF ROYALTY!* THE *ONLY* WAY I CAN *FORCE* THESE SUPERSTITIOUS DOPES TO TRAP THEIR *BELOVED* ANIMALS IS BY MY *RIGHT AS CHIEF!* WITHOUT MY *NECKLACE,* THEY'LL *DROP ME* LIKE A HOT ROCK!

GET YOUR *SPEARS* AND *MACHETES,* YOU FILTHY FOOLS! WE'LL HAVE *THREE HOSTAGES* NOW! *DEAD OR ALIVE!* AFTER THEM!

!

I GUESS WE CAN *SLOW DOWN* NOW! THERE'S NO REASON FOR THAT TRAPPER TO *CHASE US!* HE'S PROBABLY TOO UPSET ABOUT HIS *LOST MENAGERIE!*

?

SI! THAT WAS PROBABLY A *YEAR'S* WORTH OF WORK THAT WE SET FREE! WE DID *MUY BUENO,* CABALLEROS!

"THREE HOSTAGES NOW!" ~SQUAWK!~ "DEAD OR ALIVE! AFTER THEM!" ~SQUAWK!~

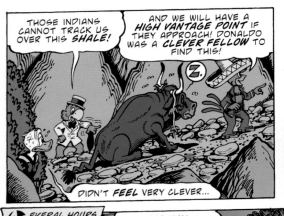

HOMINA... HOMINA... HOMINA...

THREE SHINING ARCHES ACROSS A SWAMP— THE GATES TO THE LOST CITY!

WE WANTED *ADVENTURE*, EH, COMPADRES? BUT THIS IS BECOMING ENOUGH TO MAKE ME WEAK IN THE KNEEBONES!

BUT... BUT WHERE WAS THE *CRYSTAL ROAD*?

PERHAPS UNDER CENTURIES OF GRASS?

HOLY FRIJOLE! JUST LIKE DONAL'S JUNIOR PRAIRIEDOG BOOK SAYS— A ROAD THAT *SHINES LIKE A MOONBEAM!*

DOWN BELOW IT WAS COVERED BY *LOOSE SHALE!* THAT'S WHY NOBODY *SEES* IT!

WELL, IT'S TOO DARK NOW, BUT IN THE MORNING WE'LL GO *EXPLORING!*

DONAL', DO YOU THINK WE ARE *SAFE* HERE? MAYBE THOSE INDIANS WILL FIND OUR *TRAIL?*

NO, EVEN IF WE *LEFT* A TRAIL OVER THAT ROCKY GROUND, IT'S *TOO DARK* FOR THEM TO FOLLOW *NOW!*

EVEN IF THEY LEFT A TRAIL OVER THIS ROCKY GROUND, IT'S *TOO DARK* FOR US TO FOLLOW THEM *NOW!*

WHAT? *NOW* WHAT'S WRONG WITH YOU IGNORANT SAVAGES? ARE "FOREST SPIRITS" AFTER YOU AGAIN BECAUSE I MAKE YOU *TRAP ANIMALS* FOR ME?

HUH? WHAT--

THE *SHINING CRYSTAL ROAD!* MAYBE IT'S *ALL TRUE?* THERE MIGHT *REALLY* BE MINES FILLED WITH THE MOST *FANTASTIC* JEWELS IN CREATION?

:*GASP!*:

FORGET THOSE DO-GOODERS WHO FREED MY ANIMALS! YOU DOPES ARE GOIN' INTO A *NEW* LINE OF WORK—THE *MINING BUSINESS!* FOLLOW ME TO THE *MINES OF FEAR!*

To BE CONCLUDED